KT-145-089

Sports in Action

cheerleading

in Action

John Crossingham

Illustrations by Bonna Rouse
Photographs by Marc Crabtree

 Crabtree Publishing Company

www.crabtreebooks.com

Created by Bobbie Kalman

Dedicated by Bonna Rouse
To all my sisters, for their love and support

Editor-in-Chief
Bobbie Kalman

Author
John Crossingham

Editorial director
Niki Walker

Project editors
Rebecca Sjonger
Laura Hysert

Editors
Kathryn Smithyman
Amanda Bishop
Molly Aloian

Art director
Robert MacGregor

Design
Rose Gowsell
Margaret Amy Reiach (cover)

Production coordinator
Heather Fitzpatrick

Photo research
Laura Hysert
Jaimie Nathan

Special thanks to
Doug Martin and the Ontario Cheerleading Foundation, Carley Newman, Ryan Alan, Anastasia Reeve, Heather Lloyd, Mikey Yasumura, Diana Gibb, Kaitlyn Hetherington, Travis Stirrat, Yin Xia Lu, Alexi Hetherington, Joel Balthaser and Jon Schmieder from Pop Warner Little Scholars

Consultant
Deborah Gryder, Production Manager, National Spirit Group Tim Rowland, Coach, Markham District High School Cheerleading

Photographs
All photographs by Marc Crabtree except the following:
Comstock Images/www.comstock.com: page 3
Photo courtesy of Pop Warner Little Scholars, Inc.: pages 5, 31 (bottom)
Copyright SW Productions 2003: page 4
Digital Stock: front cover

Illustrations
All illustrations by Bonna Rouse except the following:
Katherine Kantor: front cover, pages: 10 (pom-poms), 25, chapter heading on pages 4, 8, 14, 18, 20, 24
Trevor Morgan: page 7

Crabtree Publishing Company

www.crabtreebooks.com   1-800-387-7650

Copyright © **2003 CRABTREE PUBLISHING COMPANY.** All rights reserved. No part of this publication may be reproduced, stored in a retrieval system or be transmitted in any form or by any means, electronic, mechanical, photocopying, recording, or otherwise, without the prior written permission of Crabtree Publishing Company. In Canada: We acknowledge the financial support of the Government of Canada through the Book Publishing Industry Development Program (BPIDP) for our publishing activities.

Cataloging in Publication Data
Crossingham, John
    Cheerleading in action / John Crossingham;
illustrations by Bonna Rouse
    p. cm. --(Sports in action)
Includes index.
This book describes the basic skills, moves, competition, and important safety information for the sport of cheerleading.
ISBN 0-7787-0333-9 (RLB) ISBN 0-7787-0353-3 (pbk.)
1. Cheerleading —Juvenile literature. I. Rouse, Bonna. II. Title. III. Series.
LB3635.C76 2003
j791.6'4   LC 20039008231
                                                                      CIP

**Published in
the United States**
PMB 16A
350 Fifth Ave.
Suite 3308
New York, NY
10118

**Published
in Canada**
616 Welland Ave.,
St. Catharines,
Ontario, Canada
L2M 5V6

**Published in the
United Kingdom**
73 Lime Walk
Headington
Oxford
0X3 7AD
United Kingdom

**Published
in Australia**
386 Mt. Alexander Rd.,
Ascot Vale (Melbourne)
V1C 3032

Contents

What is cheerleading?

Cheerleading is a sport that combines athletic movements with team spirit. Both girls and boys can be cheerleaders. When cheerleading began 100 years ago, cheerleaders performed only at sporting events such as football and basketball games. Their job was to raise team spirit by calling out cheers.

Cheerleading has changed since then! Today, it is much more athletic, and cheerleaders no longer perform just to support other sports teams. National and regional cheerleading organizations hold competitions in which **squads**, or teams, perform routines that show off their fitness, grace, and strength.

More than cheers

Cheerleading is physical and fast-paced, and cheerleaders must be fit and well trained. Many **cheers**, or routines, involve acrobatic moves called **stunts**, as shown left. In a stunt, cheerleaders hold up and sometimes toss one or more of their teammates into the air. Stunts require strength and balance. Cheerleaders also use energetic dancing and gymnastics moves, such as **tumbling**, to make their cheers more exciting.

Get with the program

Many schools have cheerleading programs that male and female students can join. Unlike other school teams, which have seasons that last only part of the year, a cheerleading squad often practices and performs throughout the entire school year. Some cheerleading programs, such as the Pop Warner® Spirit Program, are not connected with any schools. Their squads practice routines and enter competitions year-round.

Counting on the coach

To practice cheerleading safely, you need to be supervised by a coach. **Spotters** are also important. They are coaches or senior cheerleaders who help guide your body as you learn new moves. Spotters are ready to catch you if you lose your balance doing a stunt. Many cheerleading organizations have rules to help keep the sport safe. Coaches know these rules, so follow their advice while practicing and performing.

Coaches not only help their squads with routines, but they also help build the confidence of the cheerleaders.

5

The essentials

Cheerleading does not require a lot of equipment. In addition to proper shoes, cheerleaders wear matching **uniforms** at all games and competitions. Each squad's uniform has different colors. Shirts often display the team's **logo**, or symbol, on the chest. Girls usually wear fitted shirts and short skirts. Boys wear loose tops and matching shorts or athletic pants. While practicing, cheerleaders wear comfortable clothing such as shorts and T-shirts.

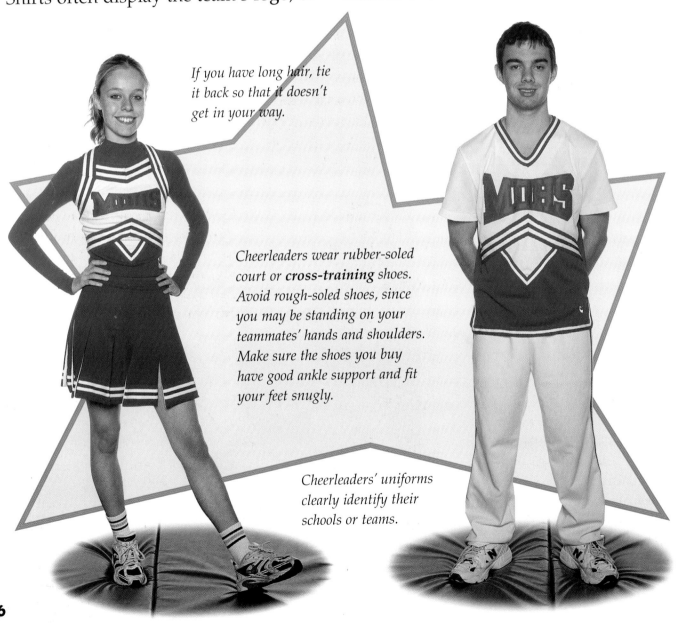

If you have long hair, tie it back so that it doesn't get in your way.

*Cheerleaders wear rubber-soled court or **cross-training** shoes. Avoid rough-soled shoes, since you may be standing on your teammates' hands and shoulders. Make sure the shoes you buy have good ankle support and fit your feet snugly.*

Cheerleaders' uniforms clearly identify their schools or teams.

Pom-poms, or poms, are brightly colored balls made of paper or plastic strips. Young cheerleaders often use them because poms can be seen easily over long distances, and they add excitement to cheers that have only a few stunts. Poms are not usually used in routines with difficult moves because they can get in the way.

Cheerleaders sometimes use large cones called **megaphones** to help **amplify** their voices, or make them louder. Megaphones make it easier for cheerleaders to be heard over noisy crowds at sporting events.

Cheerleaders don't use signs as often as they did in the past, but signs still have a place in cheerleading. They are sometimes used to encourage the crowd to make noise. The signs show phrases that the crowd can shout out to encourage the team.

Leading cheers can make you **dehydrated**, or cause you to lose moisture from your body, especially on a hot day. Be sure to have water nearby. A small snack such as fruit will also help maintain your energy.

Warming up

Before practicing any cheerleading moves, you must warm up. Begin your warm-up by moving your body. Walk or jog lightly for about five minutes and then perform the stretches shown on these pages. Do the stretches gently—you don't want to strain your muscles. Remember to breathe steadily while you stretch!

Hamstrings stretch

Stand on your left foot and lift your right leg so your partner can grab your heel. Once you have your balance, your partner will gently raise your right leg. You'll feel the stretch in the back of the leg. Keep your right foot flexed, not pointed, and your back straight. Hold the stretch for a count of ten before your partner releases your leg. Now stretch your other leg. Switch positions with your partner and act as his or her support.

Quadriceps stretch

Stand on your left foot and lift up your right foot behind you until you can grab it with your right hand. Pull gently until you feel the stretch down the front of your leg. Hold the stretch for a count of ten and then stretch your left leg.

Shoulder stretch

Stand up straight with your shoulders relaxed. Raise your right arm in front of you, keeping it straight. Bring your left arm underneath it, so that your arms meet at the elbows. Use your left arm to pull your right arm gently across your body. You'll feel a stretch in the back of your right shoulder. Count to ten. Release your arms and relax your shoulders. Now stretch the other shoulder.

Canoe stretch

Sit facing a partner with your legs straight and as far apart as possible. If you cannot stretch as far as your partner can, place your feet near your partner's ankles. Grasp each other's elbows. Keeping your back straight, lean forward until you feel a stretch in your inner thighs and lower back. As you lean forward, your partner leans back. Hold the stretch for ten seconds and then let your partner stretch.

Back arm lift

Stand with your feet shoulder-width apart. With your arms straight, clasp your hands behind your back. Raise your arms up as you slowly bend forward at the waist. Lift your head slightly. You should feel the stretch in your chest, shoulders, and arms. Hold for ten seconds. Straighten up and then repeat the stretch.

Calf stretch

Stand with one leg in front of the other. Bend your front knee but keep your back leg straight with your heel on the ground. Slowly move your hips forward, keeping your lower back flat. Hold for ten seconds. Straighten up and switch sides.

Give 'em a hand

Cheerleading is all about using your body to send a message to a crowd. The way you move your arms, hips, head, and legs helps you communicate. Several cheerleading poses are used in all routines, from the simplest to the most complex. Learning these basic poses is like learning the cheerleaders' official language. To begin the lesson, you must know the basic hand positions.

Hand-y names

Every hand position has its own name. Your coach will refer to the positions by name when asking you to perform them. The five positions are **blades**, **buckets**, **candlesticks**, **daggers**, and **knockers**. The last four positions are made using fists. Always make your fist with the thumb on the outside. Keep your wrists straight while performing these hand positions—bent wrists look sloppy!

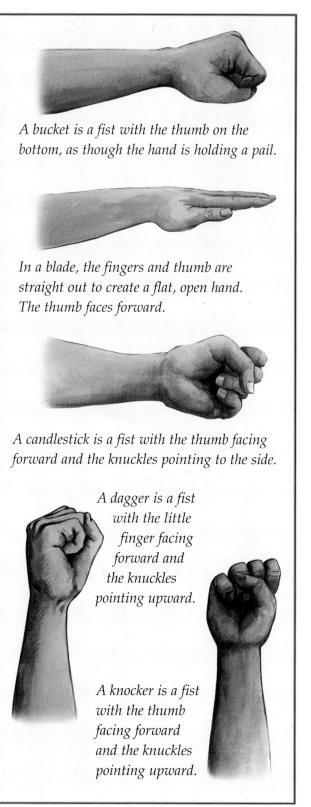

A bucket is a fist with the thumb on the bottom, as though the hand is holding a pail.

In a blade, the fingers and thumb are straight out to create a flat, open hand. The thumb faces forward.

A candlestick is a fist with the thumb facing forward and the knuckles pointing to the side.

A dagger is a fist with the little finger facing forward and the knuckles pointing upward.

A knocker is a fist with the thumb facing forward and the knuckles pointing upward.

Put your hands together

You can clap to get the crowd's attention or to help **accent**, or highlight, the beat of your cheer. In cheerleading, clapping isn't simply applauding to make noise! There are two proper ways to put your hands together—the **clasp** and the **clap**. Each one uses specific hand positions.

For the clasp, join your hands so that the fingers of your right hand go between the thumb and forefinger of your left hand. With your palms together, wrap your fingers and thumbs around so that your hands are locked.

For the clap, bring your hands together in front of your chest so that your palms are flat and touching. Your hands should line up perfectly.

Up in arms

To spectators sitting far away, your arms are the most expressive parts of your body. It's important to know all the arm positions and how to perform each one properly.

Don't move your arms loosely or lazily. Shift them sharply from one position to the next. Clear, snappy movements tell the crowd, "I'm excited, and you should be too!"

*In a **T**, both arms are straight out to the side.*

*In a **high V**, arms are straight up in a V and tilted slightly forward.*

*In a **low V**, arms are in a downward V and tilted slightly forward.*

*For a **diagonal**, one arm is in a high V, while the other is in a low V.*

*For a **cross** or **front across**, put one hand on your hip and punch the other arm across your chest.*

Arm positions

Coaches and cheerleaders often make up their own arm positions, but every cheerleader uses the positions shown on this page. Depending on what your coach decides, you can use a variety of hand positions with each of these positions. Unless the description says otherwise, keep your arms and wrists straight.

*An arm position is called **broken** if an arm is bent instead of straight. For example, this position is a **broken T**.*

*In an **L**, one arm is straight up and the other is straight out to the side.*

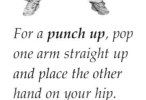

*For a **punch up**, pop one arm straight up and place the other hand on your hip.*

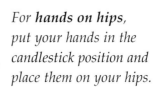

*For **hands on hips**, put your hands in the candlestick position and place them on your hips.*

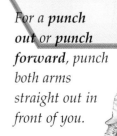

*For a **punch out** or **punch forward**, punch both arms straight out in front of you.*

13

Step into it

After learning the arm positions, you need to learn the leg positions. Girls tend to use leg movements more often than boys do. Boys often hold the same leg position throughout a cheer. Still, it's a good idea for all cheerleaders to know the basic positions. This page shows a few common leg positions.

*(left) Cheerleaders often use a **stag** at the top of a stunt.*

(right) Male cheerleaders may kneel on one leg during an entire cheer.

*For a **front lunge**, step forward with one leg and bend the knee. Keep the other leg straight. You can also do lunges to the left or right.*

*The simplest leg positions are **feet together** and **feet apart**. When apart, feet should be slightly more than shoulder-width. In both positions, legs are straight.*

High kicks

Kicks are exciting, high-energy leg movements. Cheerleaders often use them as dance moves, but kicks can also be part of **chants** and stunts. A **high kick**, shown right, requires strength, balance, and a great deal of flexibility.

Practice makes perfect

It takes a lot of practice to perfect high kicks. When you kick, your back should be as straight as possible. Keep one foot firmly on the ground during the kick. Your kicking leg should be straight and your toes pointed.

Spectacular!

When you can high kick without losing your balance, try adding arm positions. Punch ups, diagonals, and high Vs make high kicks look even more impressive!

Your coach can suggest proper exercises that will help prepare you for kicking. In order to prevent injury, remember to be patient as you practice your kicks. Perfect a simple kick before moving on to an advanced one such as the high kick.

*To do a **hurdler**, kick one leg forward and high in the air. The other leg is bent behind you.*

*For a **tuck**, pull your knees up to your chest. Hold your arms in a high V or a hands-on-hips position.*

Jump for joy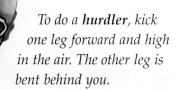

Jumps add an explosive element to any cheer. The members of a squad should try to **coordinate** their jumps, or perform them at precisely the right time. They may leap in **unison**, or at the same time, or they may jump one after another with perfectly spaced timing.

Make a point!

There are more types of jumps than are shown here, but these common jumps are good starting points. They will test your flexibility and power. Jumps are like exclamation points in a cheer, so use your legs to burst into position. Every jump has a specific body pose in midair. Snap sharply into position and hold the pose as long as possible.

*To do a **herkie**, straighten one leg and lift it high to the side. Bend the other leg behind your body. Your knee on the bent leg should point downward.*

*In a **toe touch**, lift your legs as high to the sides as you can in a splits position. Lean forward at the waist but keep your head up and shoulders facing forward. Your arms are straight and in a low V.*

Ready, set...

All jumps begin the same way, with a set of steps called the **preparation**, or **prep**. The prep looks good, and it also adds power and height to a jump.

*Now spring up into a jump such as this **spread eagle**!*

Stand with your feet together and your arms in a high V.

Bend at the knees and sweep your arms down so they cross at the forearms.

Happy landings

The final stage of a jump is the **landing**, which should be simple and clean. Make sure your feet are together. To help soften the landing, bend slightly at the knees and land on the **balls** of your feet. The balls are the soft, flat parts just behind your toes. Once you are confident in your landings, you can add an arm position such as a high V or T.

Call it out

Your voice is an important tool in getting a crowd to hoot and holler. You cannot speak as you normally would because your words must travel a long distance. You must learn how to **project** your voice so it will be heard by everyone in a crowd. Projecting is like aiming and firing your voice at a target. There are a few tricks that can help you project farther.

From the chest

Hold your hand against your throat and say something. Can you feel your throat vibrate? Now put your hand on your chest and speak. Does it vibrate too? If not, lower your voice a bit and speak louder. Now you should feel the rumble of the sound in your chest. This way of talking—called "speaking from your chest"—makes your voice travel farther.

Make it clear

Enunciation, or the way you say words, is also key. Don't let your words run together. Speak each word separately and with force. Be sure to say every syllable clearly. Finally, put emotion into what you say! If you shout the cheer with excitement and feeling, you'll be more likely to fire up the crowd.

Remember to smile and keep your voice loud and low. High-pitched voices do not travel well through the air.

To practice projecting your voice, stand about 50 feet (15 m) away from a friend and shout a cheer. See if your friend can repeat what you said.

Performing a chant

One of the simplest ways to combine the skills shown so far is in a chant. A chant is a short, peppy cheer that uses arm movements and leg positions to emphasize the words. The movements in the chant follow the **rhythm**, or beat, of the words. The rhythms are usually simple—think, "1-2-3-4, 1-2-3-4" or "1-2-3, 1-2-3." You can use your voice, clapping, and arm and leg movements to help keep the beat. Cheerleaders often perform chants along the sidelines of sports games to pump up the crowd in support of their team.

Test your spirit!

Try this chant to test your moves, enunciation, and voice projection. Remember, make all your movements sharp and crisp. Snap your arms and legs into each new position. Count out the beat before you start. Begin each new move on a beat.

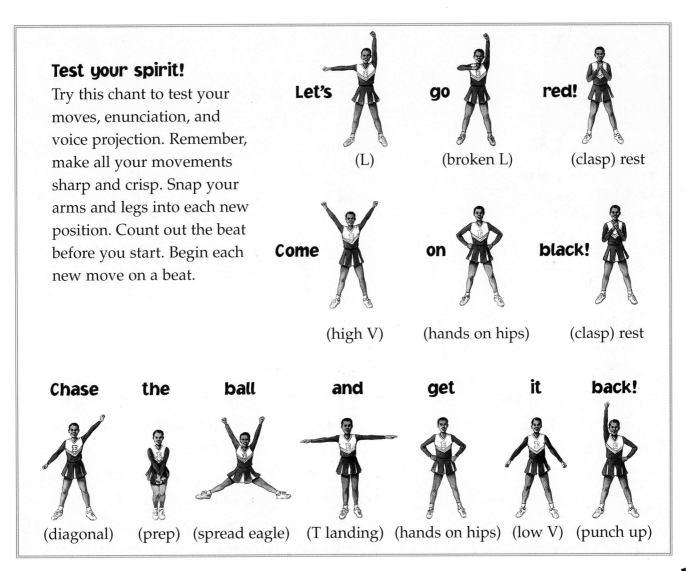

Let's (L) **go** (broken L) **red!** (clasp) rest

Come (high V) **on** (hands on hips) **black!** (clasp) rest

Chase (diagonal) **the** (prep) **ball** (spread eagle) **and** (T landing) **get** (hands on hips) **it** (low V) **back!** (punch up)

Feel the groove

Dancing is a big part of cheerleading. Cheerleaders can use all kinds of dance styles and techniques, from hip-hop to jazz. Unlike chants, dance routines focus more on smooth, fluid movements than they do on abrupt, distinct positions. Cheerleaders move continuously during a dance routine instead of holding poses on the beat, as they do in chants.

Although squads use poses such as the T or punch up in their dance routines, they also make up their own moves. A squad usually works with its coach to design a great routine full of unexpected moves. The best dance routines have two features—coordinated movement and **originality**, or a unique style.

A squad adds dance moves to its routine to make it more interesting.

Finding the perfect beat

Dances are the only routines that cheerleaders perform to music. The music they choose is very important, since it sets the tone for their routines. Most squads pick songs that are upbeat and fun because they energize both the cheerleaders and the crowd. Dance routines are usually only 30 seconds to a minute long, so squads pick the liveliest parts of the songs for their routines. At larger schools, some squads plan their dance routines to go with the songs played by their school bands.

Coaches work with their squads to design great routines. Anyone can suggest ways to make the dance exciting.

Follow the tune

There are no rules for putting together a dance routine—some of the best moves are found just by dancing for fun. Try **adapting**, or slightly changing, some cheerleading positions to come up with new moves. For example, start with a diagonal and add a high kick to it, and then spin around and pop into a punch up while stomping one foot. The possibilities are endless!

An energetic dance encourages the crowd to cheer.

Take a tumble

Many young cheerleaders are also **gymnasts**, or boys and girls who practice the sport of gymnastics. Gymnasts can make great cheerleaders. Gymnastics combines strength moves and flexibility with artistic beauty. Some gymnastics moves, such as **cartwheels** and **handsprings** (see opposite page), have also made their way into the sport of cheerleading. They add a lot of skill, movement, and visual excitement to routines. Tumbling is the act of turning your body end over end, as in a forward roll. Gymnastics tumbling also includes moves done in midair, such as **aerial** cartwheels and **back tucks** (see opposite page). Cheerleaders often perform a string of tumbling moves one after another. This string is called a **tumbling run**. Cheerleaders can change direction during their tumbling runs with **transition moves** such as cartwheels. Tumbling runs can be a great distraction while other squad members prepare for stunts.

Learn it properly

Tumbling runs are exciting additions to any routine, but they can't be learned overnight. Tumbling moves can be dangerous. Only a proper gymnastics coach can teach you how to perform them. Spotters are required to help guide your body through the moves. If you are interested in adding tumbling moves to a routine, speak to your coach.

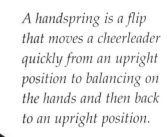

A handspring is a flip that moves a cheerleader quickly from an upright position to balancing on the hands and then back to an upright position.

The cartwheel is an important skill to learn because it leads to many other tumbling skills such as aerial cartwheels. For an aerial cartwheel, the tumbler does not put her hands on the ground.

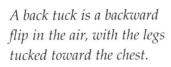

A back tuck is a backward flip in the air, with the legs tucked toward the chest.

Stunt team

Stunts are the most jaw-dropping moves in cheerleading, as cheerleaders are lifted and thrown high in the air by their teammates. Stunts require good communication between the two or more people performing them. Before you get too excited about trying stunts, take the time to master your basic positions.

Only then—and with the help and approval of your coach—should you attempt these skills. All stunts require years of training and proper coaching.

Even squads that can perform difficult stunts such as this one always have spotters standing ready to help in case someone becomes unsteady.

Top and bottom

In a stunt, there are two roles—**flyers** and **bases**. Flyers are on top. They are usually small and light since they get lifted or tossed into the air. Bases are the people who lift, hold, and throw the flyers into the air. They must be strong and stable. Most stunts use one flyer and two or more bases. Sometimes extra bases are added to act as spotters, in case a flyer falls. Flyers and bases work together to perform two types of stunts—**mounts** and **lifts**. In mounts, the flyers climb onto the bases and then pose. In lifts, the bases hoist a flyer up onto their thighs, shoulders, or hands.

Base basics:

- Have your feet at least shoulder-width apart for balance. If you're not balanced, the flyer won't be either.
- Even if you're not the main base, try to stay in contact with the flyer at all times.
- Give your flyer a short count before bringing him or her out of the stunt.

Flying high:

- Keep your knees **locked** so your legs remain straight. If your legs wobble, it's difficult for the base to hold you up.
- Straighten your back and don't lean forward or backward. Let the base balance you.
- Make your arm movements smooth, not jerky.

The thigh stand

One of the first mounts to learn is the **thigh stand**. In this mount, the flyer does not stand very high off the ground. There is little chance of injury with a thigh stand, so flyers and bases can get used to their roles without the fear of getting hurt. This mount can be done with one or two flyers.

Advanced stunts

There are many rules to keep cheerleaders safe while they perform stunts. For example, cheerleaders are not allowed to perform **full extension** stunts until they are seniors in high school.

In these stunts, the bases straighten their arms when lifting the flyers. High schools do not allow cheerleaders to perform any stunts that are more than **two high**, or two people high.

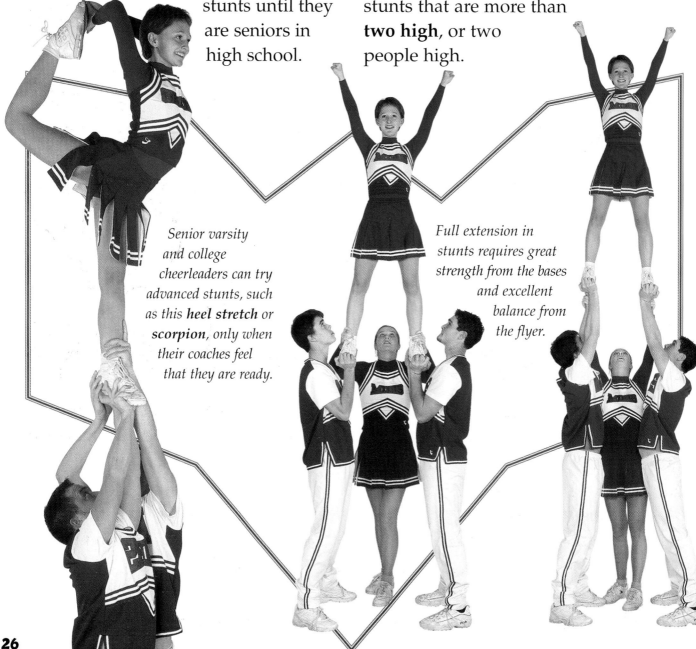

*Senior varsity and college cheerleaders can try advanced stunts, such as this **heel stretch** or **scorpion**, only when their coaches feel that they are ready.*

Full extension in stunts requires great strength from the bases and excellent balance from the flyer.

Building a pyramid

Cheerleaders are always challenging themselves to perform more difficult stunts that require more bases. Some have four or more bases for a single flyer. The extra bases act as spotters for the flyer and lend added support. A squad attempts the most famous stunt—the **pyramid**—only when the coach feels it is skilled enough. A pyramid is made up of two or more stunts that are joined together. The flyers link the stunts by holding one another's hands and sometimes legs. Some pyramids are made up of only two stunts and use six or seven people. Others, such as the pyramid above, use the entire squad and include several stunts!

Getting down

To **dismount**, or get down, from a mount such as the thigh stand, a flyer simply steps down. For most lifts, however, getting down is just as spectacular as going up. Coaches and squads want dismounts to be smooth and safe but also exciting for the crowd to watch. The most common dismount is called the **cradle**. The flyer on the left is using a cradle to dismount from a full extension stunt.

Gotcha!

For the cradle, at least two bases catch and support the flyer's back and thighs. In this dismount, the bases are also called **catchers**. The cradle must be timed well by both the flyer and the catchers. The cheerleaders agree to a countdown beforehand. It is usually, "1-2-GO!" At "GO," the bases give the flyer a slight push upward. The two main catchers then join arms, and the flyer drops down on their arms in a seated position. An extra base catches the flyer's shoulders and head if she starts to fall backward.

Pop goes the dismount

The **pop down** is a quick, simple dismount that looks great in a routine. This dismount requires three catchers. Once the bases release the flyer from the lift, she slides straight down into their arms, as shown right.

That's tricky!

Senior high school cheerleaders attempt even more daring dismounts. One such move is the **toss**. In a toss, the bases throw the flyer into the air and then catch her in a cradle. While in midair, the flyer may perform a jump such as the spread eagle.

In a pop down, the flyer's fall is slowed and guided by three catchers. The rear catcher is the most important. This person reaches up and grabs the flyer's waist as she comes down.

Performing for a crowd

Whether a squad is performing at a local football game or a national competition, it needs a great routine. The best routines combine everything you have read about in this book. Cheerleaders use chants, dancing, tumbling, and stunts to impress the crowd. Something must be happening at all times during a routine.

While some members of a squad are tumbling, for example, others are preparing for a stunt. As long as most of the squad is doing something, the audience gets the impression that the squad is continuously on the move.

A routine's final stunt uses the entire squad. Now that's teamwork!

At a game

At sports events, cheerleaders perform during pauses in the games. Some routines are short chants or dances designed to fill a quick break or time-out. The longest routines are performed at **halftimes**. They include stunts and tumbling moves designed to amaze and entertain the crowd.

Competitions

Cheerleaders also perform long routines at competitions. These routines last a few minutes. Most squads start their routines with eye-catching stunts or tumbling runs and break into chants or dances in the middle of their routines. Chants and dances are not as tiring as stunts and tumbling, so they give a squad a chance to regain its energy for the big finale. Most squads save their most impressive feats, such as giant pyramids, for the end.

How did we do?

A cheerleading squad needs to be exciting and original. Its members must move well as a group. Finally, it needs to be heard over a long distance. Judges think about all these factors when choosing the finest squad at a competition. They give awards to the best squads in several age groups.

Many squads do a group cheer before competing to build excitement before they perform.

Squads win competitions by practicing and perfecting every part of their routines.

Glossary

Note: Boldfaced words that are defined in the book may not appear in the glossary.

base A cheerleader who lifts, holds, or throws flyers into the air during a stunt

catcher A base who catches a flyer

chant A short, snappy routine that combines a shouted message with clapping, arm positions, and leg moves

cheer A longer routine involving stunts, tumbling moves, arm and leg positions, clapping, and shouted messages

coordinate To time moves perfectly so that everyone performs at the right moment

flyer A cheerleader who is lifted, held, or thrown into the air during a stunt

halftime The rest period between two halves of a sports game

landing The final position of a jump, flip, or throw when the feet touch the ground

lift A position in which a cheerleader is held in the air

lock To hold joints stiff and tight so arms or legs are perfectly straight

mount A stunt in which a cheerleader steps up onto a teammate and poses

project To direct the voice so that it can be heard clearly at a distance

spotter A person who guides cheerleaders through new moves and catches them when necessary

squad A cheerleading team

stunt An acrobatic move involving two or more cheerleaders

transition move A movement that allows a cheerleader to change direction while linking the parts of a tumbling run

tumbling A series of rolls, flips, and jumps performed one after another

Index

3 4 5 6 7 8 9 0 Printed in the U.S.A. 2 1 0 9 8 7 6 5 4